Miss Mahoolala

Author Doris DeNeui

Illustrations Dean E. Lindberg

www.deanlindberg.com

Copyright © 2017 Doris DeNeui

All rights reserved.

ISBN: 1979112894
ISBN-13: 978-1979112895

I dedicate this book to mother who gave me life – and called me Miss Mahoolala

Miss Mahoolala is very personal. She is a result of my reminiscing. Mother called me Miss Mahoolala when I was a child.

"Well, if it isn't Miss Mahoolala," she'd say. And the tone of her voice indicated whether she thought I was cute or mischievous.

I thank Dean E. Lindberg, my nephew, who drew the illustrations. He captured elements of my parents home: the old radiators, the antique tables, the fireplace with its large mirror, the open stairway, the plug-in floor lamps, and the overstuffed furniture.

Miss Mahoolala lives on in my daughter and granddaughters. Perhaps you see her in your family, too.

Doris De Neui

Miss Mahoolala
Come to our house.
She completely beguiled
My loving spouse!

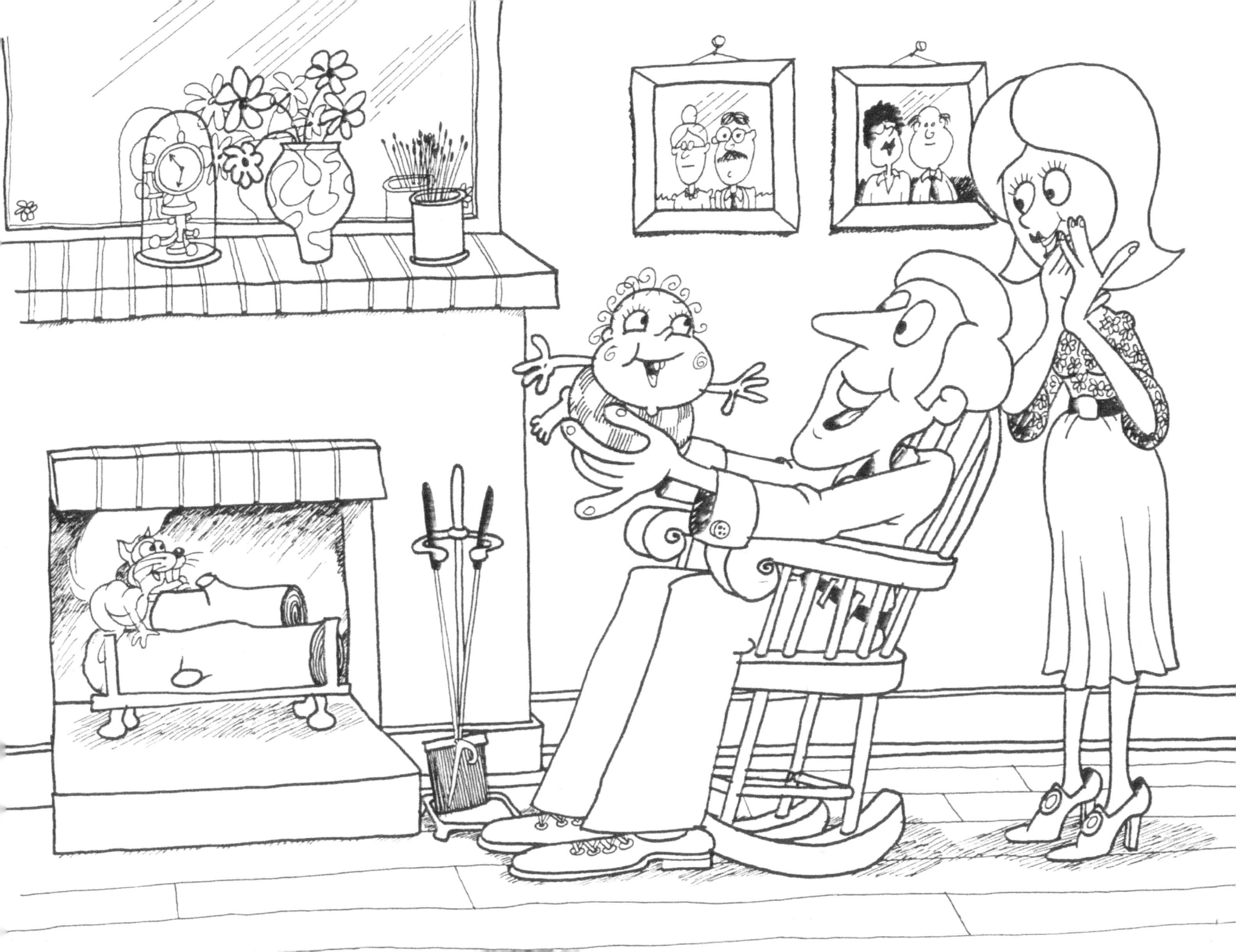

Miss Mahoolala
In her "sarong"
Keeps us enchanted
All the day long!

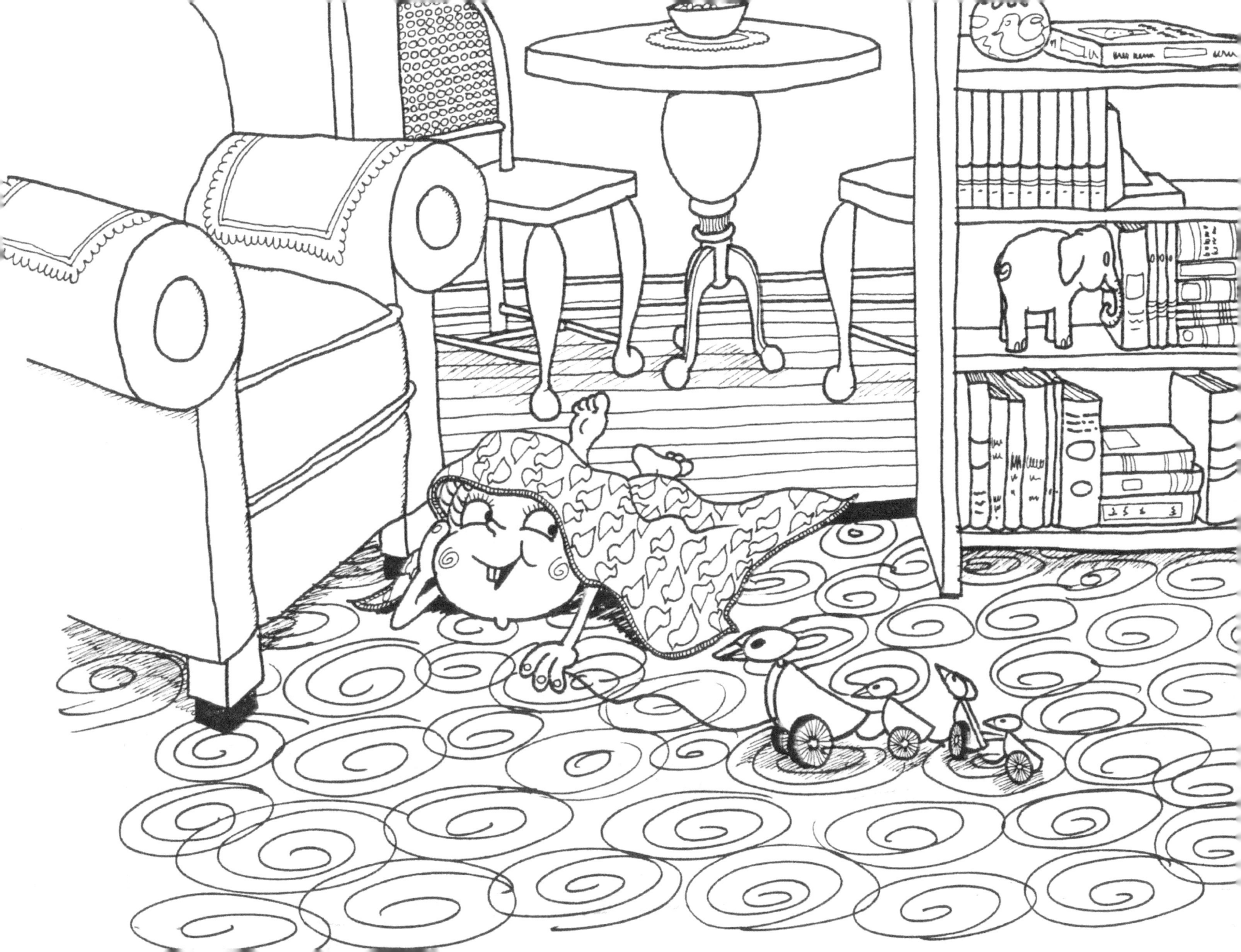

Miss Mahoolala
In ruffles and bows,
Pulled off her shoes
And played with her toes!

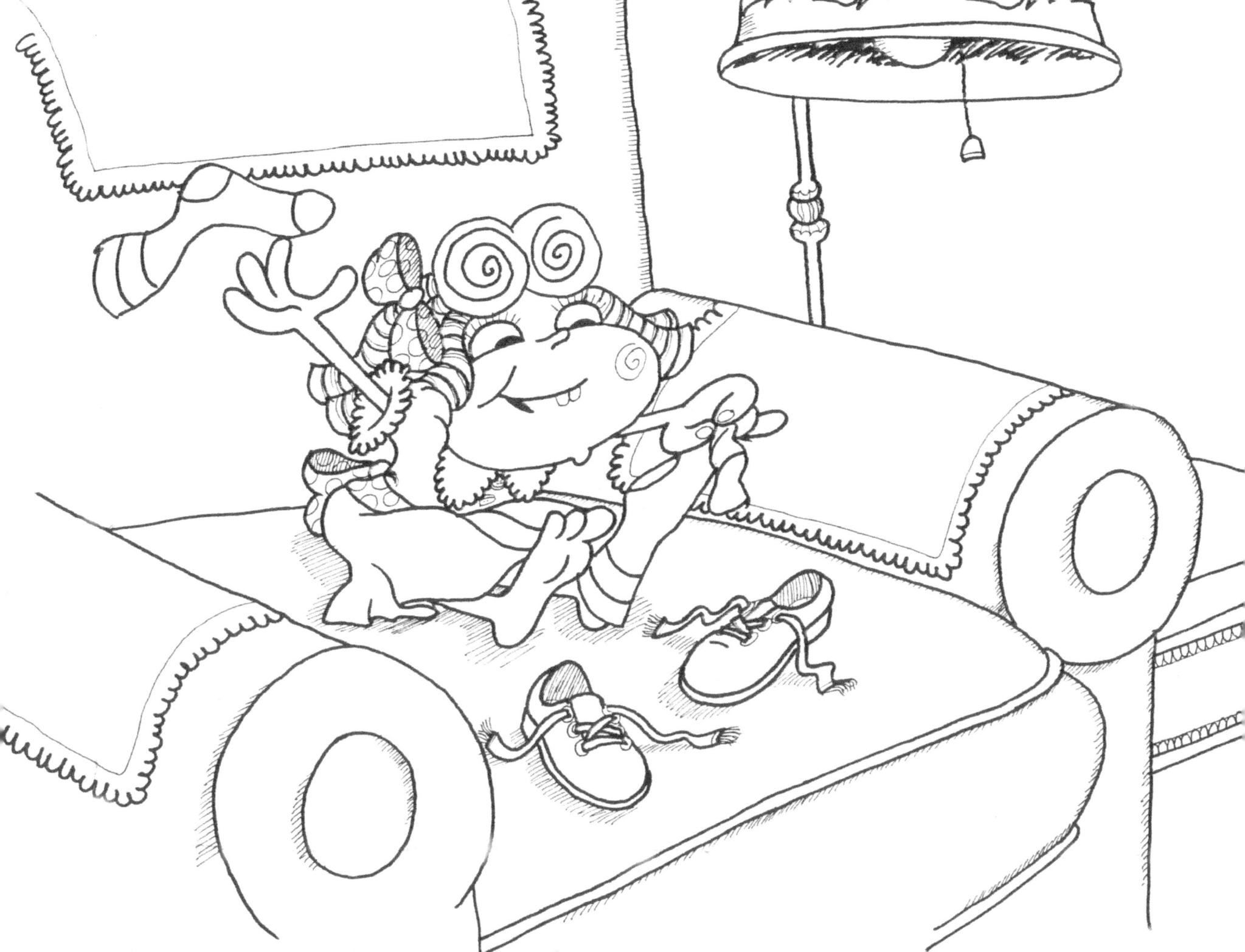

Miss Mahoolala
Is that you
Tangled in that
Pink tutu?

In this coloring book you will find some poems with no pictures.
This is your opportunity to sketch and color your own thoughts and ideas.

Miss Mahoolala
Knocked on my door.
I let her in —
She sat on the floor!

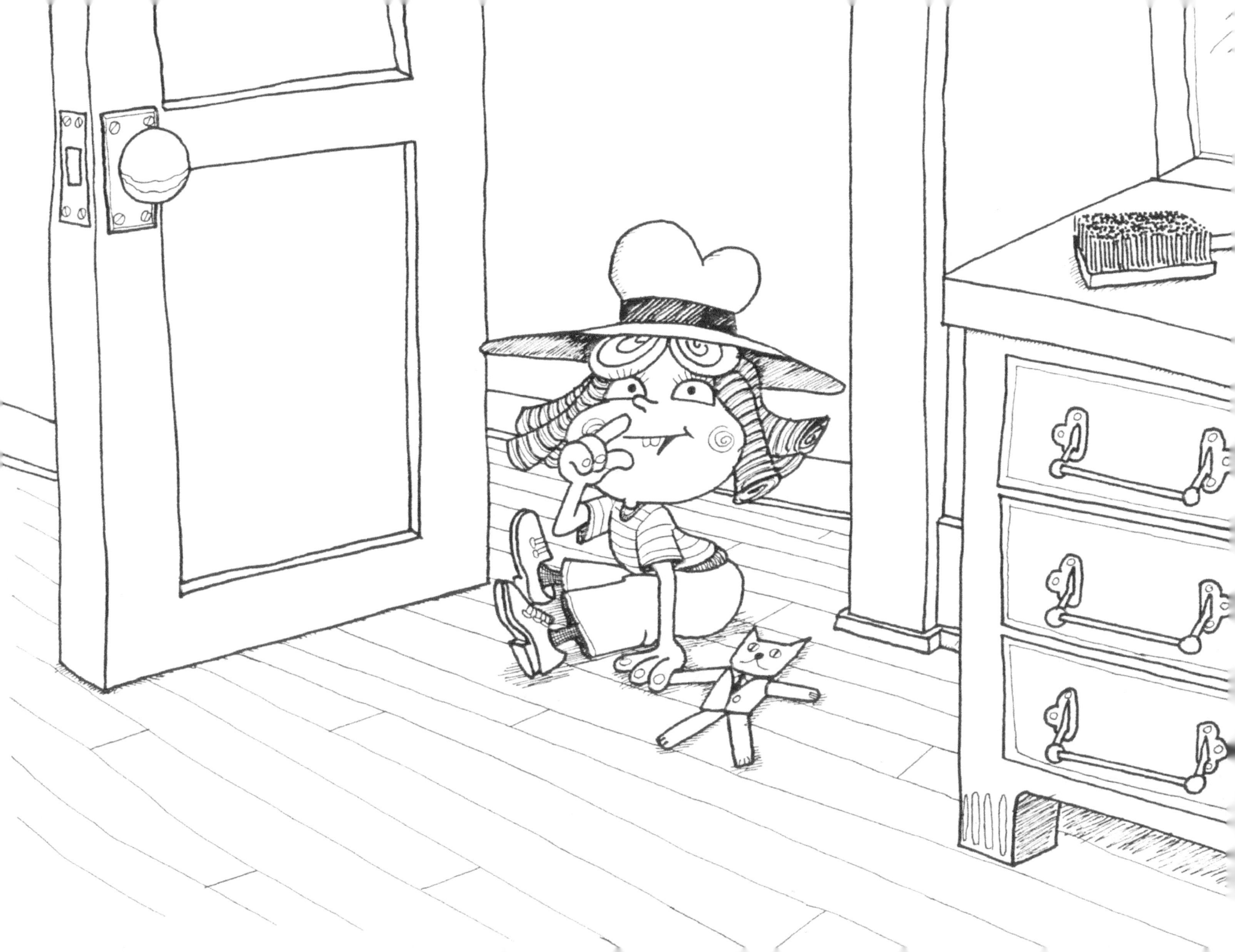

Miss Mahoolala
Spilled her milk -
It ran all over
Her satin and silk!

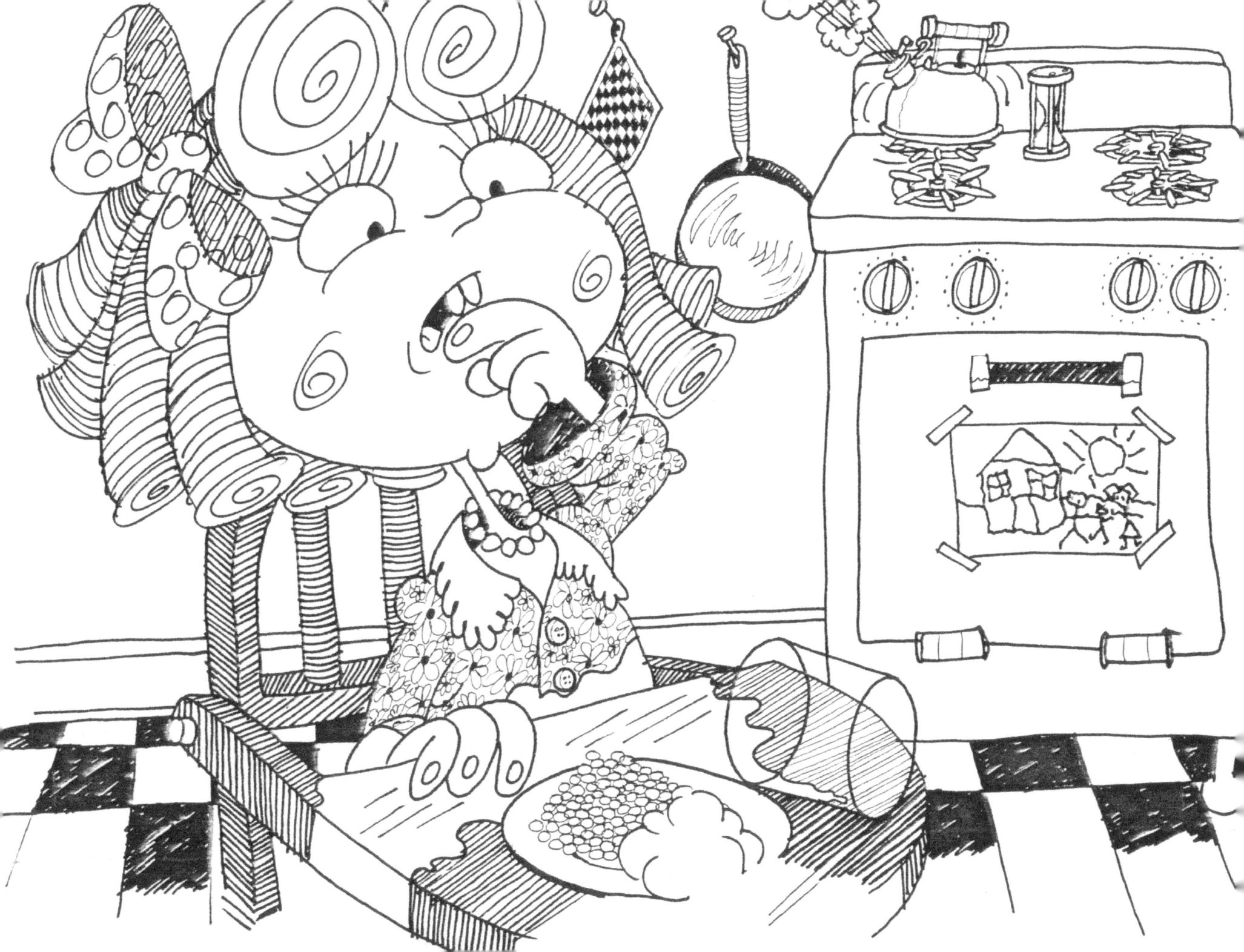

Miss Mahoolala
Dressed in lace,
With chocolate ice cream
All over her face!

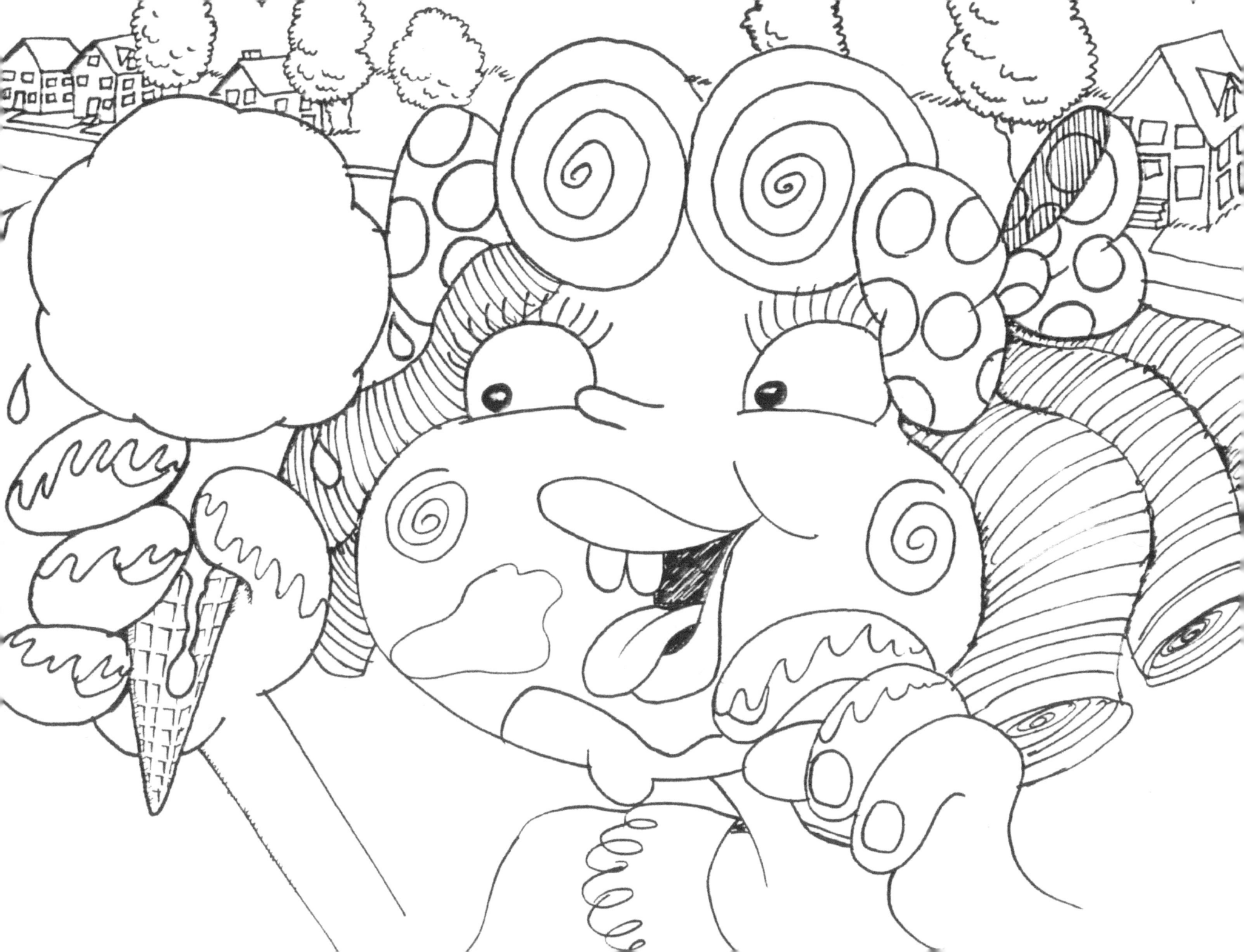

Miss Mahoolala
Looked in the glass.
What did she see?
Her mom and a loss!

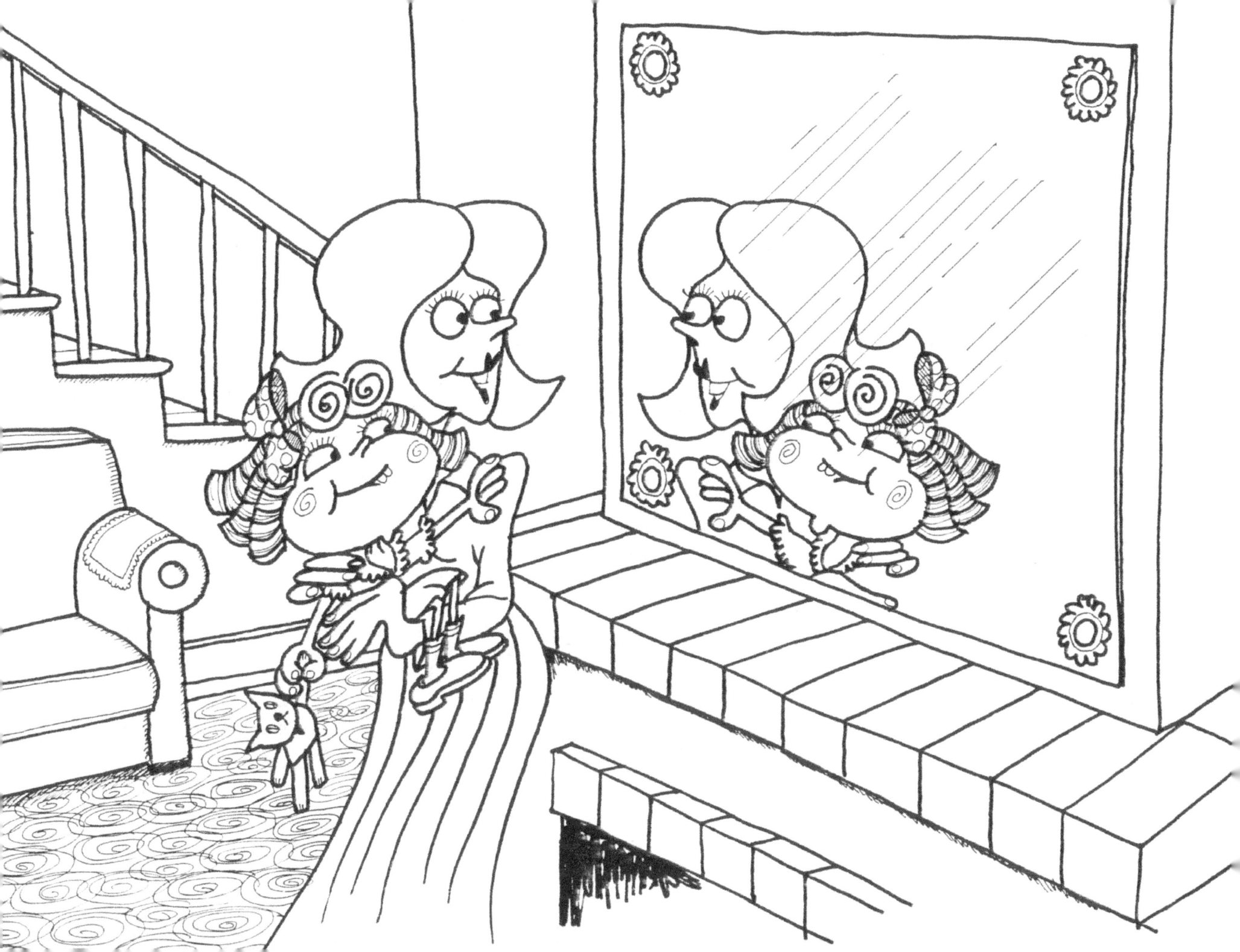

Miss Mahoolala
Having Fun
Kneading bread dough
For a cinnamon bun!

Miss Mahoolala
Trailing a drape,
Pretending she's wearing
An exquisite cape!

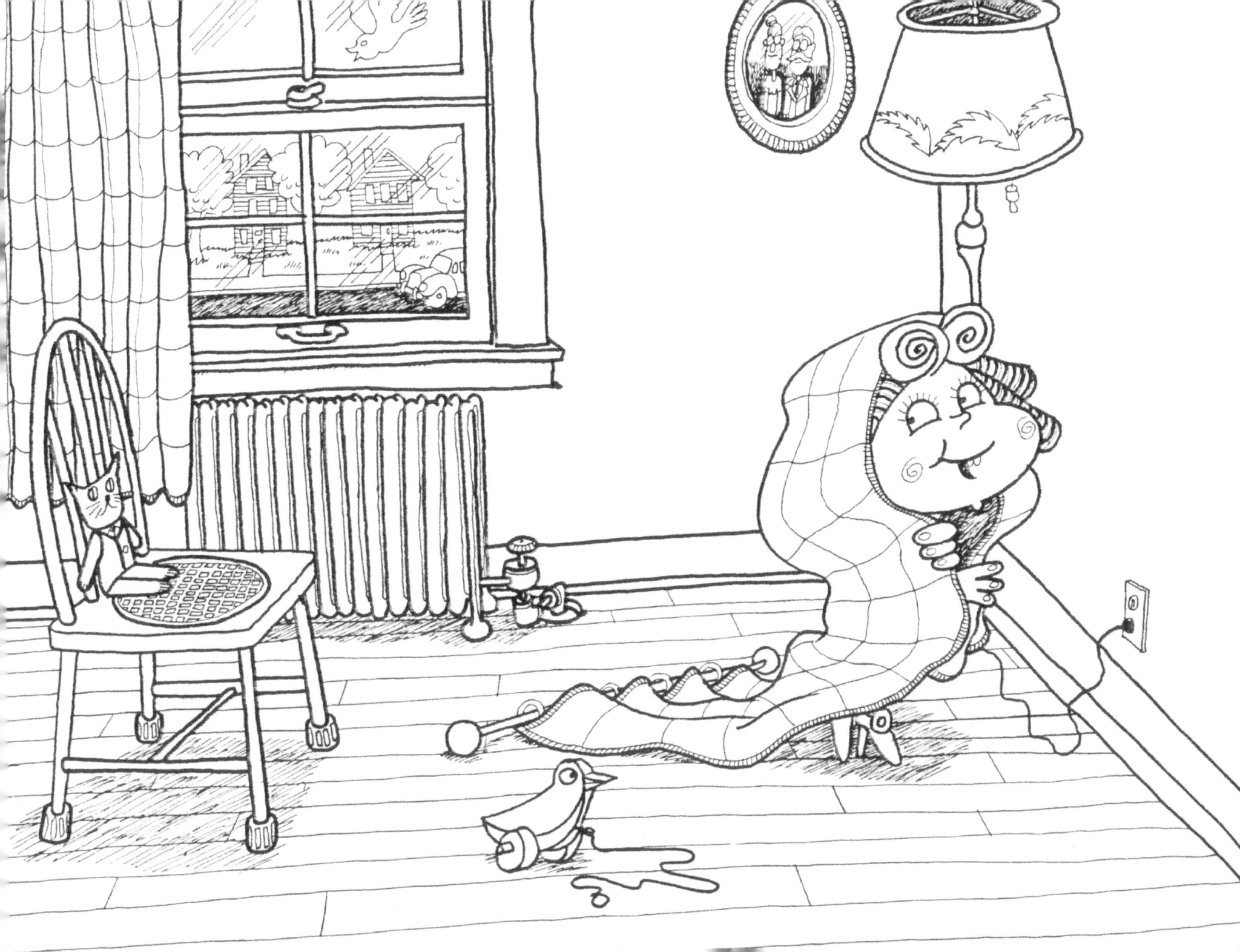

Miss Mahoolala
Come for tea
With her dad's big hat
And shoes from me!

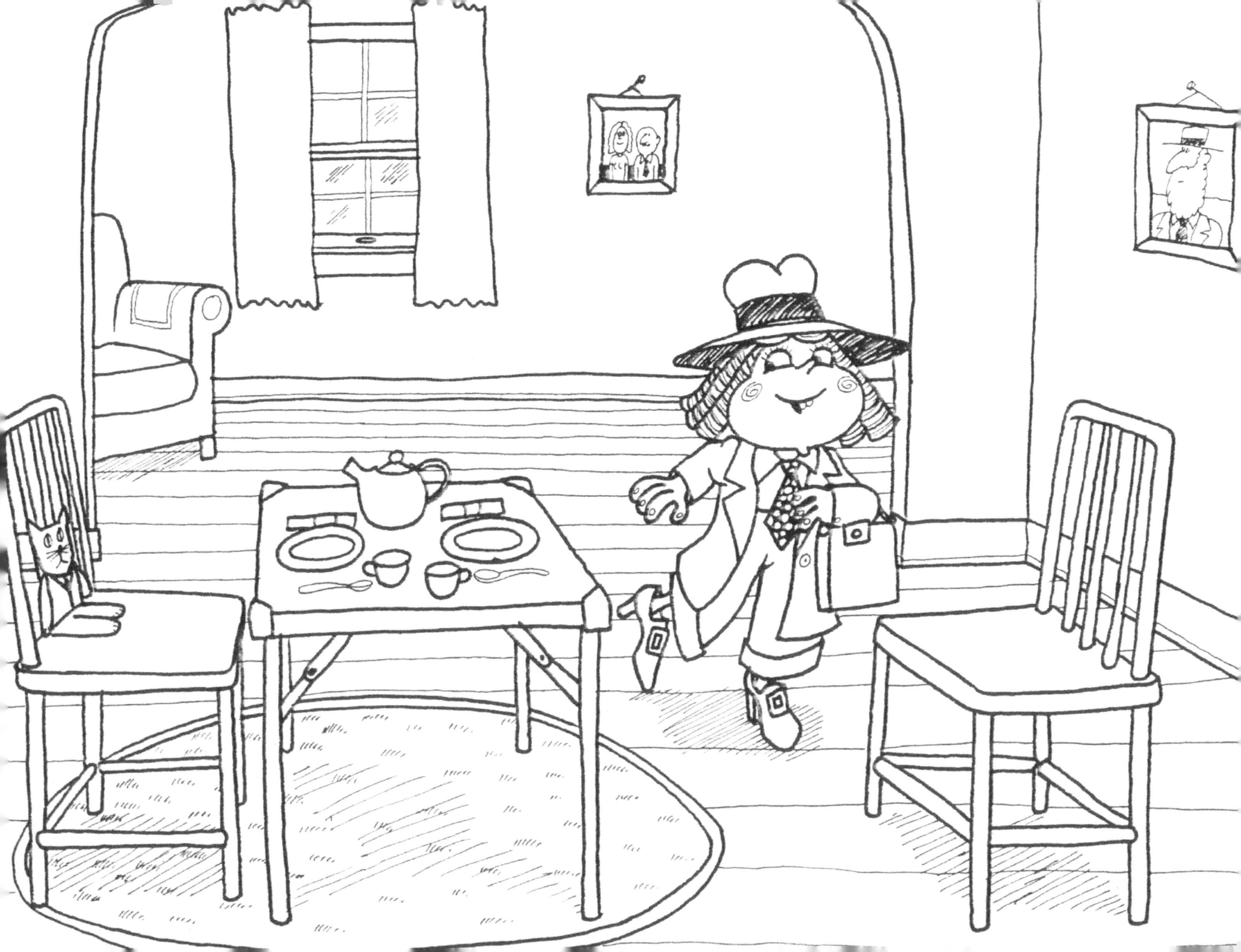

Miss Mahoolala
Closed her eyes tight.
I tucked her in bed
And kissed her good night.

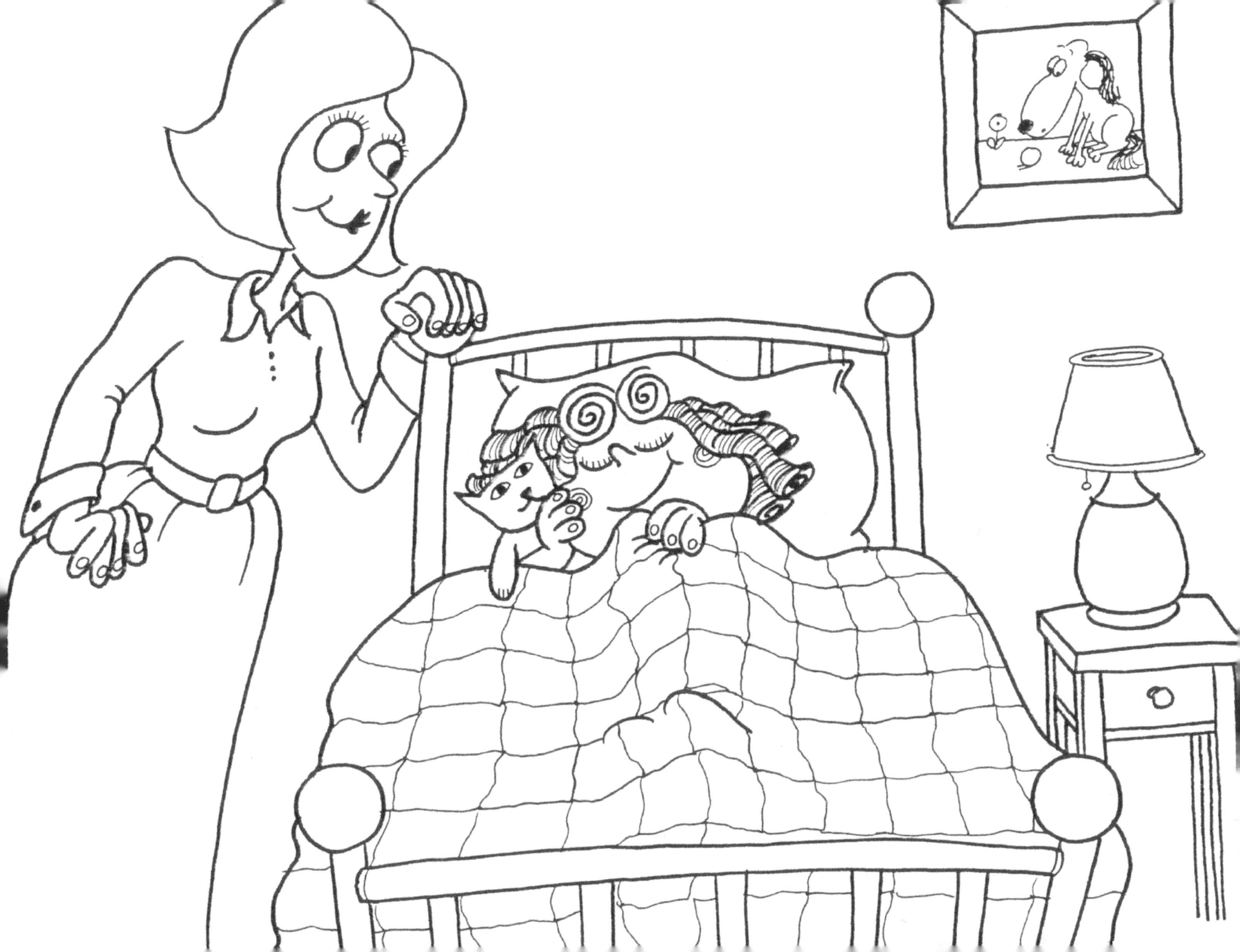

Miss Mahoolala
Has married a spouse.
Life is empty
Since she left our house.

Miss Mahoolala
Has gone away
She'll return
Some vacation day!

Miss Mahoolala
What is this?
A carbon copy
Of my little miss?